The Corporate Mute

Tiffany Gray Jackson

Dedication

First and foremost, I dedicate this work to God, my husband, my family, and my friends. Without God's hand on every page and my team's hard work, *The Corporate Mute* would not exist.

To myself: for facing fear, embracing change, and emerging stronger. Writing *The Corporate Mute* has been a personal transformation from doubt to faith, from hesitation to boldness. I am living proof that with Christ, all things are possible.

And to you, my fearless readers: though our paths may not have crossed *yet,* I hope these words make you feel seen, known, and empowered. May these stories echo through generations and remind you that you are never alone, you are undeniably *enough,* and together, we rise.

Contents

Introduction

As a little girl, I always looked up to my grandmother.

She was the most selfless and loving person I've ever known, the kind of person who would spend her last two dollars on you if she knew you needed it.

She was my world.

I was enamored of her grace, style, and integrity. I have fallen in love with scarves and pearls because of her.

My grandmother devoted her life, heart, and soul to helping others through her nursing profession. Inspired by her example, I earned my master's in public administration and dedicated my career to improving people's lives within professional environments.

For over two decades, I've held managerial positions at one of the nation's top healthcare providers, where I ensured that customer relationship management, regulatory standards, and medical and behavioral interventions were in place to secure premium healthcare quality for all.

But early in my career, I realized the corporate healthcare space was not built for people who looked like me: a highly educated, talented, driven, ambitious, and fly (did I mention fly?) African American woman.

I started keeping a mental record of incidents with colleagues and began observing common themes. I assigned personas to them as they emerged, and these incidents and observations inspired the journey of *The Corporate Mute.*

Let me introduce our guide on this journey: Ebony.

Ebony never backs down from a challenge, wins the Volunteer of the Year Award annually, loves and protects her team members at all costs, and accepts new opportunities. She is every workplace's biggest cheerleader.

How does she do it? Short answer: she fakes it while suff ering in silence as *The Corporate Mute.*

Behind the façade of perfection is no superwoman.

Ebony is a human being with faults and fl aws, longing for respect, appreciation, and support in these thugged-out "workplace streets." It's a jungle where you must shapeshift, wear many hats, and do what you can to survive.

Things can get ugly, and spoiler alert: they do.

These stories, told through the lens of Ebony's experiences, reflect the personalities represented throughout this journey while navigating the corporate workplace. Throughout this journey, I questioned myself countless times: *Who am I? How do people perceive me?Am I being fake?* I balanced these questions, roles, and personas while remaining resilient in the face of adversity. I refused to let these challenges defeat me, steal my joy, or change who I am at my core.

The Corporate Mute will take you on Ebony's journey through Freeze, Fawn, and Flight—three of the four physiological reactions the body experiences when encountering stressful situations.

We enter Ebony's story amid *The Quiet Storm*—a culmination of workplace moments that cause her to freeze. While freezing helps her survive these situations, Ebony's stories teach us how suff ering in silence can be costly to our health and wellness.

Ebony's moments of Freeze transition into Fawn as she meets the *Workplace Hype Machines*—the overly dramatic DJ Khaleds of the workplace. These are the colleagues who encourage her to people-please and sacrifi ce her sense of self to maintain peace in the workplace. Arrogant and cocky, they smile in your face but speak behind your back to leadership and everyone else. They thrive on attention and proximity to power, using hype to gain influence while exhausting everyone in the process.

Beyond The Quiet Storm and the Workplace Hype Machines lies the final stretch of Ebony's journey: *The Shift*. No longer freezing or fawning to survive, she chooses Flight as a way forward. Through intentional change, transition, and growth, Ebony rises above the madness, surpasses her own expectations, and takes flight toward a new beginning.

Ebony is not just me; she is all women in the workplace experiencing the good, the bad, and the exhaustion. As you navigate your corporate journeys, I hope you see yourselves through Ebony's not-so-rose-colored glasses and know you're not alone. I want you to find solidarity, love, and healing with other women in your workplace, because having a community that's built on trust is essential to thriving in your career and life.

Wherever you are in your workplace journey, know that Ebony and I are with you, cheering you on from the sidelines. You are unstoppable and more powerful than you know.

Trust me.

If I can do it, you can do it too.

You got this.

Part 1
The Quiet Storm
(Freeze)

Ms. Brain Fog

OH, THE INFAMOUS corporate retreat. A meeting of the minds filled with burnt coffee, cringeworthy small talk, mansplaining, and dairy overload. The motherland where the "executive landlords," as Ebony affectionately calls them, get to strut their corporate lackluster feathers and pretend they are the smartest people in the room with the most innovative ideas, stolen from their employees. Meanwhile, their teams squirm with anxiety and heavy armpit sweat as they attempt to answer every question while racing to complete their packets to 100 percent, the indicator of a "successful" retreat.

Gird your loins and let the acid reflux games begin.

It's Thursday afternoon, and after a beige and bland lunch, Ebony takes some antacids to prevent the volcano from erupting in her chest as she enters the next meeting. She sits with a colleague as Ms. Brain Fog, a poised, articulate, well-dressed, and well-liked African American account manager, enters the room. A star player on Ebony's team and in charge of over fifty accounts, Ms. Brain Fog will present after Ebony's opening remarks.

"Welcome, everyone! I hope you all enjoyed a delicious lunch and are ready to dive deep into our quarterly retreat meeting! Please follow along in your packets and leave your questions until the end. To start us out today, please welcome Ms. Brain Fog." As Ebony sits down, she is grateful she wore her favorite turtleneck, its high collar masking the stress hives creeping up her neck.

Ms. Brain Fog gives an impeccable presentation. As she is about to close, an executive landlord named Dan asks her, "Can you confirm the Erickson account total again, please? I forgot the figure you shared."

Ms. Brain Fog smiles at him and says, "I'll follow up with you after this meeting about that figure, Dan."

"Sounds great; thank you," says Dan, smirking at another executive landlord as Ms. Brain Fog happily takes her seat. Ebony observes Dan's smirk but is more focused on clapping for Ms. Brain Fog.

Two weeks later, Ebony, Dan, and a few other executive leaders are gathered to discuss the retreat meeting when Dan mentions Ms. Brain Fog's presentation.

"She was kinda rude and direct; don't you guys think? I didn't like her tone when I asked her to confirm the Erickson account. I think I may need to sit in on her meetings and make sure she's staying on task."

The other executive landlords nod in agreement.

Wait. Ms. Brain Fog has never received a complaint from a client, and she did nothing wrong! Ms. Brain Fog is the personification of elegance, class, style, and intelligence, but just because she couldn't recall *one* thing when asked, suddenly management needs to sit in on her meetings?

Disoriented and angry, Ebony's body becomes numb as she stands and addresses leadership. *Cue GloRilla and DMX.*

"You know she's expecting, right? She also just got married this year. She's juggling a lot right now," says Ebony.

Dan looks surprised. "Oh, really? How many months is she?"

How many months is she?! Really, Dan?! What in the Jerry Springer and HIPAA violations is going on here?! If Ms. Brain Fog were not a woman of color, Dan probably would have sent her an e-card and an edible arrangement by now! The audacity.

After this incident, Ebony promises herself that she will never speak up in a meeting again.

This is the precise moment that turns Ebony into *The Corporate Mute.*

She excuses herself and walks to her car to avoid confrontation. As she sits down in the driver's seat, she is startled by a news alert about the killing of George Floyd and the ensuing protests happening around the country, and the tears begin to fall.

The combined trauma of this recent executive leadership meeting, the constant pressure to be everything to everyone, and the social unrest surrounding the senseless killing of Black and Brown people proves too much for Ebony. She has finally reached her breaking point and needs help.

Ebony schedules an emergency appointment for that evening to be evaluated and learns that she is suffering from anxiety, depression, post-traumatic stress disorder (PTSD), and fatigue. On Friday morning, less than twelve hours later, she is admitted to an inpatient hospital facility.

Ms. Brain Fog is in every workplace, and with the culminating stressors of life and work, she may be on the verge of becoming a corporate mute herself. There will always be more to her story than meets the eye, no matter how flawless her pantsuit and presentation may be.

So not if, but when you encounter Ms. Brain Fog in your workplace, be an Ebony to her if you can. Whether she's your colleague or employee, encourage her and ask her how she's doing with intentionality. We need more empathy and understanding in the workplace because we will all be Ms. Brain Fog at times in our careers.

Oh, and just in case you missed it—Executive Landlord Dan had a brain fog moment *before* Ms. Brain Fog in this story. But Dan walks on water and never makes mistakes, right?

Let that marinate.

Ms. Lowball

"THE FIRST RULE of Fight Club is you do not talk about Fight Club." The second rule of Fight Club is the same. It's *that* important.

Tyler Durden's quote from the action-packed 1999 movie *Fight Club* can be applied to the corporate workplace regarding salary negotiation.

Discussing wages in the workplace feels like you're sharing your deepest, darkest secret while naked in front of all your peers. If you ask about someone else's salary, the energy shifts, doves cry, and an angel loses its wings. People look at you like you're crazy.

Proper salary negotiation is not widely taught in our society, and it's a common issue women face in the workplace. Unfortunately, we learn these skills by making mistakes.

This is precisely where we find Ms. Lowball, excitedly entering the final round of interviews for a company in the corporate healthcare industry. As a single mom, she knows that making a strategic career move like this would be best.

On a crisp Friday morning, Ms. Lowball puts on her lucky interview outfit, showcasing a pink-and-green blazer and a pearl brooch, a gift from her daughter Saree. Nervously, she enters the prestigious-looking high-rise building, passes through security clearance, and takes the elevator to the highest floor.

As she exits, she walks past a friendly face in the hallway. They greet each other with a smile, and Ms. Lowball is grateful to see a warm and inviting face that looks like hers. *Maybe one day I'll get to work with her*, she thinks.

Ms. Lowball greets the receptionist and is ushered into an executive meeting room with a large conference table where two men and two women are seated. Ms. Lowball introduces herself and takes a seat.

The hour-long interview goes well. She answers their questions confidently, and the executive landlords look impressed. They all nod at each other as they cue Janice, one of the two female executive landlords.

"Before we can officially extend an offer for the position, we'd like to discuss your salary and compensation. We can offer a base salary with full benefits, a 401(k) plan with a four-percent match, and opportunities for growth within the company. How does this sound?"

All Ms. Lowball heard was freedom, opportunity, and security. *The corporate American dream has been realized. How could she do any better than this?*

"That sounds amazing; I gladly accept! I'm honored to join your team," she says.

Over the next few years, Ms. Lowball excels. Her quarterly performance reviews are always positive, and as an incentive, the executive landlords give her a twenty-five-cent or fifty-cent raise per review.

But she hasn't been promoted or considered for other growth opportunities. Ms. Lowball's consistent raises haven't improved her overall compensation, and she notices her colleagues thriving in their positions. She feels stuck, so she decides to attend graduate school to upgrade her skills and hopefully secure a promotion.

Graduate school equips her with valuable skills, including salary negotiation and market research. She realizes she has been underpaid, overqualified, and undervalued in her current position. Although angered by this discovery, she uses her frustration as motivation to improve her situation.

Not long after graduating, Ms. Lowball receives an email stating that her departmental leadership is changing, and it includes an introduction to her new supervisor, Ebony. After reading the email, she realizes the kind face she passed in the hallway years ago is now her supervisor. This feels like divine alignment. She is about to email Ebony when she receives a desktop notification about a promotion opportunity within the company. Excited by the news, she reaches out to Ebony and schedules a lunch meeting with her for the following day.

Ebony and Ms. Lowball enjoy lunch together, and Ms. Lowball feels an instant connection with her new supervisor. Ebony is the manager she never knew she needed. Feeling energized by their conversation, she shares her struggles within the company.

"Ebony, I have lowballed myself for far too long. Earning my master's degree made me realize that I'm ready to level up and start earning my worth. Yesterday, I received a notification about a new job posting within our division, and I want to apply for it. Can you help me?"

Ebony smiles and replies, "It would be my pleasure to help you, Ms. Lowball. I can relate to your situation because I, too, had to learn how to survive and negotiate through trial and error without any assistance. Trust me, and stick with me for a year. I'll help you strengthen your skills and earn the salary you deserve."

Ms. Lowball and Ebony shake hands and begin to strategize.

Ebony schedules a meeting with Executive Landlord Dan to discuss Ms. Lowball's performance. She quickly learns that Ms. Lowball is the lowest-paid and lowest-ranking member on her team. Although infuriated, Ebony remains calm and composed as she asks Dan how this is possible.

"She was an external hire, Ebony, and she didn't sell herself in her final interview! She took our base pay and didn't ask for more, but we've given her a raise at every performance review," says Dan.

Disgusted but not surprised by the minimal effort to promote Ms. Lowball, Ebony feels it is her duty to equip her with the necessary tools and tactics for the negotiation room.

A year later, Ebony and Ms. Lowball are both promoted—just as Ebony predicted at their first lunch together. Ms. Lowball bursts into tears when she is notified. She knows she couldn't have achieved this without Ebony.

Executive Landlord Janice calls Ms. Lowball into her office to sign the paperwork, and Ms. Lowball has a déjà vu moment of her initial final round of interviews. But this time, she is ready to negotiate a higher salary. She receives zero resistance from Janice and is surprised by how easy it is to obtain her ask.

Ms. Lowball is like many women—inexperienced in salary negotiation and self-advocacy. Women are urged to take what they can get and be grateful to be in the room. When you encounter Ms. Lowball in the workplace, use your power and influence to help her. Empower her and teach her the tools you've learned by being an Ebony. This creates a ripple effect of learning and development—one that ensures more women receive fair compensation for their work and the freedom to live comfortably.

Here's the part we're not supposed to talk about: Executive Landlord Janice was the CEO's best friend, "hired" the same week Ms. Lowball was interviewed. Janice had a high school diploma and was underqualified for her position.

Remember the first rule of Fight Club?

Ms. Searching

QUEEN MERRIAM-WEBSTER, first of her name and ruler of all dictionaries, defines the word *search* as "to look into or over carefully or thoroughly in an effort to find or discover something."[1]

Urban Dictionary, written by the culture for the culture, defines *search* as "an endless conquest for something more than you have."[2]

On a hot Tuesday afternoon, we find Ms. Searching at the intersection of Queen Merriam and the culture, ready for more. She's had enough of the monotonous world of factory work. Armed with an associate's degree, she yearns for a stable yet exciting career. Determined to find a new path, she clocks out that day and never looks back.

The next morning, Ms. Searching awakes anew. She knows her grandmother, a nurse for four decades, would be proud of her for courageously pursuing a new chapter in life. Inspired by her grandmother's dedication to helping others, Ms. Searching begins looking for job openings in the healthcare field.

She quickly applies for a resource clerk position at a corporate healthcare company, and to her surprise, she is contacted for an interview. The interview goes smoothly, thanks to a friendly

---

1 *Merriam-Webster Dictionary*, "search," accessed March 12, 2025, https://www.merriam-webster.com/dictionary/search

2 *Urban Dictionary*, "search," accessed March 12, 2025, https://www.urbandictionary.com/define.php?term=search

interviewer and Ms. Searching's enthusiastic lie about attending the interviewer's alma mater for a degree in sports medicine. Ms. Searching doesn't care for sports, but she hopes her fictional class attendance will help her secure the job—and it does!

In her first week, Ms. Searching is like Halle Bailey's Ariel on land—unsteady, wide-eyed, and learning to find her footing. She is accustomed to being immersed in Black culture and had never had to code-switch until now.

Ms. Searching faces challenges using advanced computer software and learning proper phone etiquette. Her initial calls are like watching a train wreck happen in slow motion—painful yet hard to look away from.

"Oh, um, hello? No, wait! Sorry, hi! Thanks for calling [healthcare company]! How can I … um … help you?" says Ms. Searching with a nervous laugh.

Moments like these are precisely why she wears black daily—to mask the anxiety and moisture that surfaces throughout the day. She notices stares from passing colleagues as she wipes the sweat off her upper lip. Ms. Searching grabs a piece of computer paper to fan herself after slamming the phone down. *Of all places, must I sweat on my upper lip, Black Jesus?! Come on now, help a sista out!*

Thankfully, toward the end of her first week, Ms. Searching's supervisors—executive landlords George and Kim—observe her potential and become her trusted mentors.

After a year of working as a resource clerk, Executive Landlord Kim encourages Ms. Searching to return to school for her bachelor's degree. Though insecure about the idea, Ms. Searching trusts Kim's belief that taking this next step is necessary for her growth.

After earning her bachelor's, Ms. Searching pursues her master's degree and is encouraged by George to apply for the company's leadership program. Now armed with both degrees, Ms. Searching is promoted within the company. She is finally using her God-given gifts—helping and connecting with others and making a difference in her community—and she is getting paid her worth. But she yearns for more—to establish her own professional identity, independent of George and Kim. She is in search of a new chapter. Again.

Ms. Searching applies for a new role within the company—a decision she later comes to regret. Over the next two decades, she holds many different positions within the organization. Despite her success, the job she truly loved most was her role as a client liaison under executive landlords George and Kim.

George and Kim have always been in the background cheering her on. They even encourage her to apply to work within their division again, but Ms. Searching declines. She is frozen in her insatiable need to impress others, achieve more, and earn more money. But over time, Ms. Searching realizes that her income isn't as important as her authenticity and happiness.

Ms. Searching is not problematic. Like Ebony, she constantly wants more. But you'll be on a perpetual search for fulfillment until you find your authentic self. Remember to embrace the unexpected and step outside your comfort zone.

You are enough, just as you are. Find joy in your journey as you continue your path of self-discovery.

• • •

Professional Development
for the Corporate Soul

Imagine a world where you are fearless in asking for what you need—whether that's a higher salary, a better work-life balance, or more support. How does that version of yourself feel? If fear of rejection or discomfort has kept you frozen in place, what is one small action you can take today to help you move forward?

> "Just because you have a nightmare
> doesn't mean you stop dreaming."
> —JILLY FROM PHILLY (A.K.A. JILL SCOTT)

Part 2

Workplace Hype Machines

(Fawn)

Ms. Secretary

ON SEPTEMBER 11, 2001, two hijacked commercial airplanes crashed into the Twin Towers of the World Trade Center in New York City. A third plane struck the Pentagon in Arlington, Virginia, and a fourth crashed into a field in Somerset County, Pennsylvania. Approximately three thousand people lost their lives that day.[3]

A 2021 Pew Research Center survey of U.S. adults found that 93 percent of those aged thirty and older say they remember exactly where they were or what they were doing when they first heard the news of the September 11 attacks.[4]

In the chaotic and uncertain weeks that followed 9/11, all flights were grounded, leaving airports deserted and travelers stranded in foreign countries.

This state of anxiety and displacement is where we find Ebony—wrapped in a weighted blanket and sporting a tropical hat, with a plate of jerk chicken in her lap—as she watches the news from her hotel room. She awakens on September 12 disoriented, praying the events of the day before were only a dream. Instead, the nightmare

---

3 National September 11 Memorial & Museum, Module 1: Events of the Day, accessed March 24, 2025, https://www.911memorial.org/learn/resources/911-primer/module-1-events-day

4 Hannah Hartig and Carroll Doherty, "Two Decades Later, the Enduring Legacy of 9/11," Pew Research Center, September 2, 2021, https://www.pewresearch.org/politics/2021/09/02/two-decades-later-the-enduring-legacy-of-9-11/

continues when she receives an emergency email informing her that her flight had been canceled until further notice. Her three-day weekend getaway suddenly turns into a vacation that may never end.

Ebony panics. *Until further notice?! I have zero vacation days left!*

Ebony feels her cortisol rising as an email appears on her phone screen from Ms. Secretary, checking in on the health and safety of all within her division. Ebony smacks her teeth and rolls her eyes. She doubts the email's sincerity, given that Ms. Secretary had never shown her kindness. *Does she genuinely care, or is this an email sent on the executive landlords' behalf?*

Meet Ms. Secretary, the sickeningly sweet and sassy mama bear queen of the corporate healthcare administrative space who calls everyone "sweetie" and has the utmost trust of the executive landlords. She is the heartbeat of the office, and she knows everyone's secrets. You'll want to be on her good side. Trust me.

Ebony knows she has to contact Ms. Secretary. But what will she tell her? *Think Ebony, think!* Maybe that she is, well... uh, sick? *Yes, that's right, I'm sick!*

Ebony practices coughing and her most convincing hoarse voice as she dials the number slowly.

"Good afternoon, Ebony. How are you holding up, girl? Are you and your family okay?" says Ms. Secretary.

Ebony pauses with fear.

"Hello?"

Ebony fills the silence with her well-rehearsed coughing. "Hello, Ms. Secretary. *Cough, cough.* I'm not feeling very well. I'm not going to make it into the office today. Could you please let my supervisor know?"

"You sound awful. I'm so sorry you're sick, Ebony. I'll let your supervisor know. Take good care of yourself today, and get some rest, sweetie."

"Thank you," utters Ebony hoarsely.

Ebony receives flight delay notifications for the next two days and continues to let Ms. Secretary know that she is still unwell and unable to come to work.

The weekend arrives, and Ebony can finally attempt to digest the tragic events of this past week and strategize a plan. But due to exhaustion, she sleeps.

On Monday morning, she knows it's time to be honest with Ms. Secretary. After all, she's the only person who can help her. Ebony dials her number.

"Good morning, Ebony. Are you feeling better today? What time can we expect you in the office?"

"Ms. Secretary, I need to tell you something…"

"What's going on?"

"I'm stuck in Jamaica! I didn't get my vacation days approved, and I don't know when I can travel back to the U.S. because they keep canceling all the flights! Shit!" Ebony sobs.

"Okay, Ebony, calm down. Here's what I'm going to do. I will inform your supervisors that you have a severe flu and will be out this week. Hopefully, that'll give you enough time to get back here, okay?"

Ebony is pleasantly surprised by Ms. Secretary's kindness and discretion. But can she trust her? Ebony hopes and prays for the best as she walks to the hotel bar to order a piña colada to calm her nerves.

Ms. Secretary keeps her word, but her promise is short-lived. Ebony flies in from Jamaica on Friday morning. While she's in the friendly skies, Ms. Secretary arranges a virtual meeting with the executive landlords to reveal the truth about Ebony's absence. Ouch.

Ebony arrives at work the following Monday feeling refreshed and energized. Before heading to her office, Ebony stops by Ms. Secretary's desk to give her a hug, a danish, and a coffee.

"Thank you so much for having my back," whispers Ebony.

"How sweet of you, Ebony; thank you! Oh, before you get settled, the executive landlords would like to see you in the conference room. Welcome back!"

Ebony is filled with gratitude as she enters the conference room, but the energy in the room shifts as she sits down. As Ebony is about to speak, Ms. Secretary enters and takes a seat across from her.

Executive Landlord Janice addresses Ebony. "Ebony, it has come to our attention that your absence was not due to sickness but rather to being stranded in another country. We wish you had told the truth. Lying to us was the wrong way to handle the situation."

Ebony apologizes tearfully. "I didn't know what else to do. I'm sorry. These past few weeks have been incredibly stressful."

Ms. Secretary confidently inserts herself into the discussion. "I had to tell them the truth after I knew you were safely on your way home, Ebony. I felt ethically obligated to do it, even though you advised against it. But don't worry, sugar plum. You're not getting written up or fired or anything crazy like that. I just strongly suggested to the C-suite that we speak to you upon your return about the importance of honesty in the workplace."

Ebony's thoughts race as she replays the events of the past two weeks, including her phone calls with Ms. Secretary. *What a backstabbing bitch. I should've known better than to trust her. I'm thankful I didn't lose my job, but I want my coffee and blueberry danish back, ho.*

Ms. Secretaries are the backbone of every corporate workplace. They are the gatekeepers, the holders of information and access. To succeed in the corporate world, you must inevitably work with them.

But no matter how much they smile in your face and plan immaculate lunches for everyone's birthdays, their allegiance will always be to the executive landlords. It's important that you not cross Ms. Secretary or get on her bad side, because if you end up in a situation like Ebony's, where you are "funkin' for Jamaica," as Tom Browne's hit song featuring Toni Smith so eloquently states, you may not be so lucky.

It's time for a dance break, y'all! Sometimes we have to dance to find joy during hard times and shake off negative energy to reclaim our collective spirit.

Look up "Funkin' for Jamaica" and turn your volume UP! Hit it, Tom Browne and Toni Smith!

Feel free to continue to the next story once your Ebony-approved *Soul Train* line concludes.

Ms. Compliment

I KNOW YOU just finished your *Soul Train* line, but close your eyes.

But Ebony, I'm reading right now, duh!

I am aware, okay smarty-pants? Just read this first part, or have a friend read it, and stay with me.

Again, your eyes are closed. Imagine yourself on a beach by the water or in whatever setting you feel most relaxed.

Bliss personified.

Just as you're about to doze off to sleep, a horsefly buzzes in your ear and darts in front of your face, barely missing your mouth.

You turn into Afro Samurai, angrily trying to kill that sucker, but it just won't leave you alone.

Exhausted and annoyed, you head to the store to buy some bug spray, just in case the demon fly or any of its cousins decide to follow you home.

Now open your eyes.

You're pissed, right? Me too!

Well, keep that bug spray handy and your eyes open, because if that annoying fly were a person, it would be Ms. Compliment. She craves attention and recognition, and when she receives it, she can't get enough.

Ms. Compliment is buzzing around the office on a Thursday morning, inserting herself into everyone's business, as usual.

Much like Ms. Secretary, Ms. Compliment seeks respect and admiration from the executive landlords. On this particular morning, she's excited to inform her colleagues of a meeting she's arranged with the executive landlords to discuss her new and innovative ideas for office workflows and guidelines.

She shares her news with a nearby colleague who is on a Zoom call. "Hey, Ebony! Did you hear about my upcoming meeting? I have so many new ideas to make our workplace more efficient!"

Ebony looks up at Ms. Compliment, rolls her eyes, points to her screen full of Zoom squares, and returns to her Zoom call.

"Oh, my bad, Ebony! Have a great Zoom meeting. I'll let you know how the meeting goes!" She power-walks away, leaving Ebony shaking her head and sipping her coffee.

I have a feeling this will not end well for any of us, Ebony thinks.

Before her meeting, Ms. Compliment steams her blazer with a portable garment steamer kept in her cubicle. The steamer is obnoxiously loud, so everyone knows when she's using it. "I'm ready!" exclaims Ms. Compliment as she glides to the executive meeting room.

The executive landlords appreciate her innovative suggestions for workflow efficiency. However, they remind Ms. Compliment that she needs at least 80 percent approval from her colleagues, those implementing her suggestions, before they sign off. Ms. Compliment is disappointed by this news but sees it as another opportunity to impress her supervisors.

"No problem. I'll send everyone an email and promise them lunch and a life-changing presentation!" Ms. Compliment shoulder-shimmies from the meeting room to her desk.

After she sends the email, all of her colleagues' computers chime at once, signaling the arrival of her message. She winks at anyone who will make eye contact with her and gives them a cringey thumbs-up.

"I take it the meeting went well, Ms. Compliment?" says Ebony.

"It sure did, Ebony. You'll see tomorrow! Bring your appetite and a notepad!"

The next day, Ms. Compliment arrives at work early to set up the conference room for lunch. Ms. Secretary, the award-winning snitch from our previous story and Ms. Compliment's bestie, gladly helps her set up the room with beverages and confirms her massive lunch order from a swanky restaurant. Ms. Compliment wants her colleagues to be talking about this lunch for a while. She soon finds out they will be, but not for the reasons she thinks.

Ms. Compliment's coworkers arrive at the conference room and are surprised to find a delicious upscale buffet. Ebony smirks as she walks in. *Are we being bribed or poisoned? Let me keep my emergency contacts up on my phone just in case.*

Once everyone is seated, Ms. Compliment begins her presentation. Just minutes in, her colleagues begin to look insulted and confused. People start raising their hands and interrupting her.

Ms. Compliment is getting nervous. "Please hold your questions. We only have a limited amount of time, and I want to cover everything!" she says skittishly.

A male colleague interjects. "I'm confused. We've already done more than half of the things in your presentation. Did you look at our progress reports or project milestones before making this presentation?"

Ms. Compliment looks like a deer in headlights. "Get some more food. I'm almost done! I'll get to that!"

She realizes she's blown the presentation as she watches her colleagues file out of the conference room one by one. "Did you guys at least enjoy the lunch?" says Ms. Compliment quietly as she sinks into a chair with her head in her hands.

Devastated by the now-empty room, she dramatically bites into a garlic roll and reflects on what's transpired. Ms. Compliment knows she has lost any chance of receiving the executive landlords' approval. Her intentions were good—she wanted what was best for the team—but she failed to include them in the planning, making her colleagues feel undermined and overlooked.

In the days that follow, it's clear that Ms. Compliment's colleagues have not forgotten her presentation. Whispers fill the hallway whenever she walks by. But this only motivates her to work harder.

Later that year, she is offered a management position in another department, but the executive landlords ask her not to accept, explaining that they need her. Ms. Compliment is thrilled to be needed by the executive landlords, so she declines the position.

But is she ever promoted or allowed to advance after she stays back? Nope.

The executive landlords want to keep the "fly" in a jar—contained, controlled, and at their disposal. Here's the thing about keeping a fly in a jar: after a while, the fly sees the jar as its home, and anything outside it feels foreign. It becomes its safe space, even though there is far more to explore and discover outside the jar.

Ms. Compliment's "jar"—the corporate workplace under the direction of the executive landlords—made her forget who she was.

Don't be like Ms. Compliment and lose sight of the value you bring to every room you occupy. Folks around you may hate on you for shining bright like the diamond you are, but that's their problem.

Not yours.

Fuck a compliment.

Your impact is your legacy—not other people's opinions of you.

Ms. No-Degree

DID YOU EVER struggle with test anxiety as a kid?

I did.

I would study so hard for tests for days! But when the test got into my hands, I would freeze, knowing damn well I knew the answers!

Meanwhile, Veronica, a random fellow student, always bragged about being a good test taker despite never studying.

An A+ for Veronica and a C for me.

It felt so unfair, and I was envious of her because it felt like she didn't have to work for her success.

I soon realized that while hating on Veronica offered temporary relief, it wouldn't magically elevate my test scores. Test-taking just wasn't my ministry.

However, I worked hard to improve and eventually conquered my test anxiety.

Lesson learned.

But little did I know that this experience would follow me into adulthood in the corporate workplace.

Let me introduce Ms. No-Degree #1 and Ms. No-Degree #2.

They are present-day Veronicas who created nontraditional pathways to success, leaving the haters and innocent bystanders in the dust on their way to becoming executive landlords.

Both women work at the same company as Ebony, and she watched them transition from customer service representatives to team leads, supervisors, managers, and ultimately vice presidents.

Ms. No-Degree #1 and #2 have been with the company for twenty years, and they have worked their asses off. Their colleagues are proud of them, and so is Ebony—but it's hard for many to believe they achieved this level of success without a degree. Ebony has a master's degree and some of her colleagues hold PhDs, yet they couldn't figure out where they went wrong—or where Ms. No-Degree #1 and #2 went right.

Maybe they have just been blessed and highly favored? Let the church say amen?

Ms. No-Degree #1 and #2's consistent success brings insecurity to many of their colleagues. But Ebony admires these women, who remain emotionally strong and dedicated to their work while still managing to have a life, care for their families, and participate in company activities.

They are polished, poised, and flawless—and they play the game well... or so it seems.

One Friday afternoon, Ebony stops by an educational symposium taking place at her worksite. She looks forward to listening to some innovative lectures and catching up with a few colleagues.

As Ebony enters the event, she signs in and is greeted with a vendor bag. An hour goes by before she receives a phone call from Ms. No-Degree #1 asking her to leave.

"Hello?"

"Hi, Ebony. Are you at the educational symposium right now?"

Ebony suddenly locks eyes with Ms. No-Degree #1 from across the room and wonders why she felt the need to call her instead of coming over to chat.

"Ummm, yes, hi. We are looking right at each other," she says.

"Haha! Indeed, we are. Well, I hate to do this, but I need to ask you to leave. This is an invitation-only event, and you weren't on our list of invitees."

Ebony is appalled and embarrassed. An executive landlord she looked up to is suddenly treating her like a stranger instead of a respected team member.

Ebony bites her tongue to avoid cussing Ms. No-Degree #1 out.

"I was not aware this was a closed event. I was greeted and welcomed at the door without any trouble. I'll head to my office now."

"Thanks so much. Nothing personal!"

Ebony walks out of the event calmly, then gets in her car and screams. She has never felt more undervalued, unappreciated, and disrespected in her life.

Ms. No-Degree #2 comes from the same crock pot of pettiness and disrespect.

A few months later, on a Tuesday morning, Ebony is helping with last-minute setup for an Educational Day she has been planning for months. The purpose of the event is to facilitate in-depth conversations with subject matter experts on corporate healthcare policies and workflows.

Ebony is in her element.

She is the ultimate relationship builder, connector, and organizer, which is why she is consistently praised for organizing these types of events. Kudos, Ebony!

But when Ms. No-Degree #2 arrives at the event midday, she behaves as though Ebony never publicized the event. She even has the nerve to call her manager, the chief medical officer (CMO), to complain about Ebony. Ridiculous.

Ebony pays her no mind; she's too busy managing a successful event to notice Ms. No-Degree #2's green face of envy scowling at her from the corner of the room.

Ebony receives a call from Ms. No-Degree #2's manager at the end of the day.

"Hey!" Ebony says as she answers the call from the CMO.

"Hi, Ebony! I've heard that Educational Day was a success! Nice work. Before your next event, could you please ensure that all the executive landlords are copied on your announcements and confirmations? Ms. No-Degree #2 asked me why she wasn't informed about Educational Day, even though I'm not sure how she missed the emails and various media outlets advertising it. Just a note for you. Job well done!"

"Oh, okay. Got it! Thanks!" says Ebony as she rolls her eyes.

Ebony's supervisor is frustratingly nonconfrontational, with no interest in calling out the behavior of Ms. No-Degree #1 and #2—or the Mean Girls, as Ebony has begun to refer to them. *So much for her supervisor having her back. Sigh.*

These events happened around the same time Michelle Obama uttered the infamous phrase "When they go low, we go high," and Ebony got tired of hearing it. *Respectfully, how much higher do I need to go, Michelle? I'm exhausted!*

In my opinion, people like Ms. No-Degree #1 and #2 go low because they didn't take the traditional route to success and feel they have something to prove. They get an adrenaline rush from their elevated status and from competing with peers who are often more qualified. Their goal? Proving you wrong—and they will, even if it makes them look bad.

The Veronicas, the Mean Girls, and the Ms. No-Degrees will all show up in different ways throughout your career and get on your nerves at every corporate-level job.

Your job is to let your colleagues be great, or not, and keep it moving.

Your shine and how you show up in your work are what matter most.

Ms. People-Pleaser

AFTER A LONG WORKWEEK, there's nothing better than a Netflix and chill night with your partner, fur baby, or favorite weighted blanket. A frozen mango margarita in one hand and a slice of pizza in the other? Chef's kiss.

No matter your preferred streaming network, have y'all noticed the increased number of cult documentaries on your queues? Maybe you initially felt like your creepy neighbor hacked your account and researched cult leader classics on your dime.

Just me? Okay cool. Well, anyway, we now know that cults have been part of global society for centuries.

I'm fascinated by ex-cult members' stories and how easy it can be to wind up in a cult. It seems so obvious when we are on the other side of the television screen, right? We think, *Hey, girl, you're in a cult, GET OUT! Run, Forrest!*

But it's unfair to judge, because our lives and stories are complex and nuanced.

No matter the type of cult, I've learned from Netflix University that one of the key strategies cults use to gain followers remains the same: identify vulnerable people who feel isolated and offer them a sense of belonging within a group of like-minded people. Then, [insert infamous mack daddy cult leader of choice here] manufactures hope and a bright future through their "blueprint to a successful life" by way of calculated manipulation and intimidation—and boom. You've got yourself a cult.

When the formula is this simple, you can see why cults have the potential to pop up anywhere, even within the corporate workplace. The executive landlords have cultivated a cult-like following—a breeding ground for employees to do their bidding. This keeps leadership from getting its hands dirty, both literally and figuratively.

Keep this in mind as we meet the executive landlords' most true-blue wannabe honorary corporate cult member—the Southern belle, the Ms. Scarlett O'Hara of Ebony's office: Ms. People-Pleaser.

Articulate, charming, and hardworking, Ms. People-Pleaser avoids conflict, which makes her a doormat who struggles to say no. But lucky for her, she is best friends with her supervisor, an executive landlord named Joseph, whom she trusts to look out for her and her family's best interests without question.

Joseph rewards Ms. People-Pleaser's loyalty and overtime with Apple watches, preferential treatment, and other perks, while Ms. People-Pleaser uses her city traffic court connections to get Joseph out of parking tickets, picks up his dry cleaning, and does everything in between.

They take care of each other. A lucrative friendship.

On a Wednesday afternoon, Ms. People-Pleaser is giving a presentation when she receives a phone call from her husband. Unable to answer, she lets it ring.

Moments later, a text message appears:

"PLEASE CALL ME NOW. IT'S IMPORTANT."

Ms. People-Pleaser quickly excuses herself from the conference room and runs into the hallway to call her husband. Joseph follows to offer moral support.

She dials his number, and he answers right away.

"Hi, honey."

Ms. People-Pleaser closes her eyes and braces herself. "What's wrong?! Are you okay?"

"Due to budget cuts, the company laid off half the staff today, and I was one of them. I'm sitting in my car in shock. Twenty-five years down the drain."

Ms. People-Pleaser's hands start to shake. Joseph, concerned, puts his hand on her shoulder.

Aware she's not alone, Ms. People-Pleaser maintains her composure. "Honey, I'm so sorry. Take some deep breaths. I'll ask my mom to pick up Matthew from school. We will figure this out together. Everything will be okay. I love you."

"I love you too. You and Matthew are my world."

Tears roll down Ms. People-Pleaser's face as she clears her throat to respond. "You are my world too. I'll see you soon."

Ms. People-Pleaser ends the call and takes a deep breath. Joseph asks if he can hug her, and she gladly accepts, filling him in on her husband's news as they embrace.

Joseph ushers Ms. People-Pleaser to his office, hands her a water bottle, and motions for her to take a seat. "I'm so sorry about your husband. What a punch to the gut after working at a company for over two decades. I'm here for you guys, okay?"

Tears roll down Ms. People-Pleaser's face again as she grins and takes a big gulp of water. "Thank you, Joseph. I am lucky to have you as a friend and supervisor. I don't know what I'd do without you. The only thing I ask is that we keep this news between us."

Joseph puts his pinky finger out in front of her, and they both laugh.

Pinky promises are their thing.

"Pinky promise, Ms. People-Pleaser. Your secret is safe with me, always."

Ms. People-Pleaser joins her pinky finger with his. "You're the best, Joseph."

A few days later, on Friday afternoon, Ms. People-Pleaser is preparing to leave work early to pick up Matthew when Joseph interrupts her.

"My apologies. I know you're about to get Matthew, but could you stay back a minute? Executive Landlord Natalie wants to discuss an event she needs help with. I told her you wouldn't mind, seeing as how you could benefit from overtime right now…"

Joseph's casual mention of Ms. People-Pleaser's deeply personal matter shocks her, but aware that any hint of ingratitude would trigger his passive-aggressive behavior and worsen her work environment, she controls her reaction.

"I'd be happy to meet with Natalie. Thank you, Joseph."

Joseph claps and gives Ms. People-Pleaser a high-five. "Fantastic! It shouldn't take more than fifteen minutes. Natalie, come on in!"

They meet on Joseph's office couch for the next hour. *So much for fifteen minutes*, thinks Ms. People-Pleaser.

She's over an hour late picking up Matthew, and she knows he'll be upset. *But he'll understand*, she thinks. *He always does.*

Despite the previous week's anxiety and stress, she looks forward to the weekend with optimism. Sunday is Ms. People-Pleaser's favorite day of the week because it is strictly reserved as a family day. She gets to spend the entire day with her favorite guys.

The day usually begins with her and her husband cheering Matthew on at his flag football game, followed by lunch at their favorite diner and a walk in the park before returning home.

The Sunday following her husband's layoff feels more needed than any other Sunday they've spent together as a family. She knows they need some joy and a sense of normalcy.

While at Matthew's game, she and her husband rise to their feet, cheering as Matthew scores a touchdown. That's when she receives a phone call from Joseph.

"Hey, girl! Happy Sunday!"

"Hi, Joseph! Is everything okay?"

"Yes, I'm sorry. I know it's family day! Yay!"

Ms. People-Pleaser and her husband sit down as the game continues, and he stares at her while she listens to Joseph.

"I was just thinking about more ways to help you guys, and I started staring at my lawn! I've neglected it for weeks, and I remembered you raving about your husband's landscaping skills! Could he come over today and mow the lawn and fix a lightbulb I can't reach? I'll pay him handsomely, and we could all hang together! It'll be Family Day 2.0 at my house. What do you say?"

Ms. People-Pleaser cringes as she listens to Joseph's request.

She takes a deep breath and, with a forced smile, says, "Family Day 2.0 at Uncle Joseph's sounds great! He would be happy to help."

Family Day 2.0 with Uncle Joseph is anything but that.

Long hours, a broken lawn mower that her husband has to fix before mowing the lawn, cold pizza, sour lemonade, and Matthew napping on Joseph's couch.

Despite the exhaustion of everyone else, Joseph seems proud and energized by the opportunity to assist "a family in need."

After five hours of work, Ms. People-Pleaser's husband screws in the final lightbulb in Joseph's ceiling fan as Joseph writes him a check.

"Thank you so much for your hard work today! My yard looks immaculate. I'm sorry I took you guys away from family day, but I hope Family Day 2.0 at my house didn't disappoint!"

Ms. People-Pleaser hugs Joseph.

"It was a great day, Joseph. Thank you for thinking of us. See you tomorrow!"

The car ride home is silent, mostly because everyone is sleeping. It wasn't the family day they needed or wanted, but at least she's continuing to keep the peace at work.

The next morning, Joseph shows off pictures of his new lawn to fellow executive landlords. Ms. People-Pleaser finds out through a colleague and is mortified.

"Hey, Ms. People-Pleaser! I'm sorry your husband lost his job, but it looks like he has a promising career mowing lawns! I'd love his number!"

Ms. People-Pleaser ignores her colleague and storms into Joseph's office.

"Hey, Ms. People-Pleaser! People are pumped about your husband's lawn skills. I'm racking up some business for you guys!"

"Joseph, I asked you to keep my business between us! My husband was an engineer, for crying out loud; he's not a gardener, and he will not be going into business for lawn care! You're my friend, and I love your generous heart. But please keep my business to yourself... pinky promise?"

Joseph smiles at Ms. People-Pleaser with a tight grin and blank stare as he reaches his pinky finger toward hers. "Pinky promise."

It's the blank stare and pinky promise, for me. *Run, Ms. People-Pleaser!*

From our perspective, it's easy to see what a manipulative and intimidating executive landlord Joseph was toward Ms. People-Pleaser.

She sacrificed her sanity to please an executive landlord who held her family's future in his hands.

Executive landlords rely on gaslighting and intimidation tactics to maintain control.

But they need you more than you need them.

We need to break their generational cult-like following in the corporate workplace.

Don't be like Ms. People-Pleaser. She never left her toxic workplace—but you can.

Listen to your intuition and plan your exit strategy. Your health and well-being are far too precious and important to sacrifice over toxic behavior and a paycheck.

No job is worth the cost of your peace.

• • •

Professional Development
For the Corporate Soul

Think about the people in your professional circle. Who can you count on to give you honest feedback, support your growth, and have your back when things get tough? What qualities do these individuals share—and how can you nurture these relationships without slipping into fawning behaviors, such as people-pleasing or prioritizing others' needs over your own?

> "I say if it's going to be done, let's do it. Let's not
> put it in the hands of fate. Let's not put it in the
> hands of someone who doesn't know me. I know
> me best. Then take a breath and go ahead."
> —Anita Baker

Part 3
The Shift
(Flight)

Ms. Event Planner

DO YOU REMEMBER the infamous corporate work retreat from Ebony's first story?

You know, the one where Ms. Brain Fog couldn't recall the answer to an executive landlord's question mid-presentation and, as a result, almost got fired? Yeah, that one. Well, get ready for the ridiculousness to continue, y'all.

Let me introduce you to the corporate work retreat's stylish, louder, older cousin: the mandatory corporate work event.

Attending mandatory corporate work events can feel torturous in a way that differs from corporate work retreats.

Amid the endless vendor booths, the robotic conversations, and the sausage-measuring contest between nationally recognized executive landlords, the goal is to get in and out with as many vendor bags (for groceries) and pens (for your office) as possible before the terror starts.

But if you're lucky, every once in a while you come across a corporate event that pleasantly surprises you.

This event feels thoughtfully curated and organized, from the check-in table to the food, décor, vendor placement, programming, and entertainment.

You enjoy yourself so much that you want to mingle and experience all the event has to offer because the atmosphere is positive and genuine.

These artfully crafted experiences are Ms. Event Planner's

specialty, and she organizes them regularly for the corporate healthcare company where she works.

Ms. Event Planner has been planning events for over ten years and is consistently recognized for her work by the executive landlords. She has a passion for organizing premier healthcare symposiums and curating the best baby showers, birthday celebrations, and more.

But she would not be able to execute such events if it weren't for her award-winning events team. They are like Ms. Event Planner's soulful backup singers, two-stepping with her on the two and four count.

One Friday morning, the executive landlords call an impromptu meeting with Ms. Event Planner to discuss budget changes for the upcoming health educational symposium. She grows concerned as she takes her seat.

Executive Landlord Dan clears his throat and scoots up his chair. "Thanks for meeting with us on such short notice, Ms. Event Planner. We know you and your team have your hands full with planning our upcoming symposium."

"You're welcome, Dan. What's going on?"

"Inflation and market volatility have been kicking our butts the past few weeks. Therefore, our $100K budget for the symposium needs to be reduced to $25K. But you always make magic happen for our events, and you make it look easy! We know you'll be fine."

I'm not Jesus; I can't turn water into wine, thinks Ms. Event Planner. Although annoyed, she knows her response needs to be calculated.

"Event planning is far from easy; it is an art. However, having an adequate budget makes planning much easier for me and my team to execute a successful event. $25K will barely cover the catering and marketing materials, let alone the speakers and their travel."

Dan nods his head in agreement. "This brings me to my next point. We'd like for you to start negotiating contracts with vendors. You are their first point of contact, so why not negotiate pricing so we can get better deals?"

Ms. Event Planner places both hands on the armrests of her chair.

"Negotiating contracts is not in my job description; I have a team for that. I will write a brief report this weekend discussing the goals and objectives of event planning. Adding contract negotiation to my list of duties is not the answer."

Ms. Event Planner is proud of herself for advocating for her position and team.

Meanwhile, the executive landlords, disgusted and unhappy, stare at Ms. Event Planner for a beat.

Executive Landlord Janice breaks the silence. "A report won't be necessary, Ms. Event Planner. We thank you for your time and feedback today. As stated, the budget will now be $25K. Please reach out to us if you have any questions. Thank you."

"Thank you, Janice," says Ms. Event Planner.

Irritated and exhausted, she's relieved it's Friday afternoon; she can go home after this disastrous meeting and not return until Tuesday.

Ms. Event Planner takes Monday off for a doctor's appointment. She's grateful for the three-day weekend to work on her report for the executive landlords. They're getting that report whether they like it or not.

Ms. Event Planner spends all day Saturday writing her report. She completes it Sunday afternoon and schedules it to be sent to the executive landlords on Monday at 8:00 a.m. When they receive it, they call a meeting with the Procurement Department to validate her findings.

The Procurement Department confirms that everything mentioned in her report is accurate and that she's proceeding with the event planning process correctly. However, the executive landlords refuse to accept her data as truth.

Executive landlords don't like being proven wrong, and let's just say, *humility* is not a word often found in their glossary of terms.

Therefore, when Ms. Event Planner arrives at work on Tuesday morning, she receives a calendar invite for a follow-up meeting with the executive landlords and her supervisor for later that afternoon.

My report must've struck a nerve if they needed to invite my supervisor. This should be interesting.

Ms. Event Planner's supervisor is conflict-avoidant, readily agreeing to anything the executive landlords propose to keep meetings short and stress-free. But she hopes he will have her back and advocate for her today. Wishful thinking.

Ms. Event Planner enters the conference room where executive landlords Dan, Janice, and two others are already seated. Silence fills the room until her supervisor enters, a bit disheveled. He drops a folder on the floor and dives to retrieve its contents.

He's more jittery than I thought he would be, thinks Ms. Event Planner as she leaps out of her chair to help him. He assures her that he's fine and takes a seat.

Executive Landlord Janice smiles at Ms. Event Planner's supervisor and nods at him before officially greeting the room. "Good afternoon. Are we ready?"

"Yes," Ms. Event Planner and her supervisor say.

"We have reviewed your detailed report, Ms. Event Planner. Although not needed, it was very informative. We met with the Procurement Department yesterday to confirm your information, and we observed that you haven't been following the appropriate event planning process standards. Therefore, we'd like you to submit all your vendor contracts from 2023 through 2025 and break down the processes you took with each one in an Excel spreadsheet."

A bead of sweat rolls down her supervisor's face. Ms. Event Planner knows she'll need to speak first.

"Respectfully, Janice, I have been organizing events for this company for over ten years. I have always followed the proper guidelines and standards, and I work closely with the Procurement Department for every event. I do not have time to submit my contracts from the past two years. We have an event in two months."

"I understand that, Ms. Event Planner, but—"

Janice is cut off mid-sentence by Ms. Event Planner's supervisor.

"I'll get the spreadsheet to you by the end of the week, Janice. Ms. Event Planner has a full schedule, so I'll handle it."

Ms. Event Planner looks at her supervisor with a puzzled expression on her face.

"How about this," Ms. Event Planner says. "Instead of submitting the spreadsheet, starting today, I'll send every invoice and scope of work from our vendors to you for approval and sign-off. Is that a happy, healthy compromise for you guys?"

Dan smirks at the other executive landlords before responding. "That won't be necessary, and it sounds tedious. Corporate event planning feels a lot like wedding planning, but without the cake and booze. Can't we just get cheaper vendors that are still high quality? Oh, and we've been looking at other venues for the health symposium. We'll talk about that next."

Ms. Event Planner does a full circle spin in her chair, then stops and stares at Dan.

"Other venues?! Our event is in eight weeks! I'm willing to do whatever it takes to make sure this event goes smoothly, even go to the Dollar Store for decorations if needed, but what I will not do is disrespect our longtime vendors by underpaying them or trying to negotiate a lower price. We have worked with many of them for over a decade, and they deserve respect and fair compensation. Respect and trust go a long way in the event planning business, and I will not let our reputation suffer due to cutting corners."

Janice nods. "We appreciate your dedication and loyalty to our company and vendors. Let's keep the venue as-is for the upcoming symposium and work with the vendors we have already confirmed. Work your magic. But after this event, we will regroup and improve your event planning processes. A happy, healthy compromise, right?"

Before Ms. Event Planner has a chance to respond, her supervisor, who looks like he has just fallen into a dunk tank of sweat, rises to his feet. "Thank you, Janice. That sounds like a great compromise. We look forward to our next meeting."

Deep sigh. Wow. Ms. Event Planner was an army of one in that meeting. She had to speak for her supervisor, educate the executive landlords, and advocate for herself and her vendors' hard work all at once.

Yet she maintained her brilliance, strategy, self-respect, and truth amid adversity and called bullshit when she smelled it.

Unfortunately, in the corporate workplace, there will be a multitude of people—executive landlords and all—who will encourage you to take the path of least resistance. But in truth, it is the path that prioritizes their comfort at your expense.

Like Ms. Event Planner, be prepared to unapologetically defend your role and job description when faced with cutting corners and "staying on budget."

And when you've had enough and there is no more room for compromise?

Move on.

I know it's not always that easy, but give yourself grace and permission to create your own unique path.

Opportunities await on the other side of fear.

Ms. Christian

IF YOUR CHILDHOOD was anything like mine, you grew up in the church, and Sundays belonged to *the Lordt*—Southern twang for "the Lord"—and Sunday dinners. The down-home Southern Sunday playbook.

I come from a rich family legacy of pastors and deacons, meaning that three-hour church services (at minimum), paper-thin communion wafers and grape juice, surprise peppermint candies from the pocketbooks of elders, and Sunday school have been in my blood for generations.

The Black church is my home.

It is where my church village raised and molded me right alongside my family members.

But Sunday school? That was my sweet spot.

Was your Sunday school teacher sweeter than freshly made sweet tea on a hot summer's day, and could she charm the morning dew right off a honeysuckle? Mine certainly was, and her name was Ms. Berry.

I loved her. Ms. Berry was soft-spoken, kind, encouraging, and compassionate.

She had a gift for making Bible stories resonate with our everyday lives, sparking critical thinking through her engaging delivery. I never met another woman like her until I met Ms. Christian, the Sunday school teacher the corporate workplace never knew it needed until she gracefully glided through its golden gates on her cloud of King James Version Bible verses.

Ms. Christian was the director of operations in the same department as Ebony Monday through Friday, and on Sundays, she was the first lady (pastor's wife) of a church and a Sunday school teacher.

Her work cubicle was adorned with biblical quotes, a framed portrait of two sets of footsteps in sand, and prayer cards for her colleagues "in need."

Ms. Christian was a generous friend to everyone. But when the executive landlords would call her into their conference room, she would immediately spread office gossip.

To put it plainly, she was fake.

If you received one of Ms. Christian's blessed prayer cards, you can now use it as a coaster for your beverage as we get into her story. You'll need it.

One brisk Monday morning, Ms. Christian is working with her operations manager, Catherine, to approve statements of work (SOWs) for multiple vendors related to a few upcoming events. This approval process has been part of their Monday routine since Catherine was hired years ago as Ms. Christian's successor.

Catherine is almost done approving the large folder of SOWs when she comes across a vendor she doesn't recognize. "Ms. Christian, could you please confirm this vendor for me? I don't think he is on our pre-approved list."

Ms. Christian walks over and smiles. "You are correct, Catherine. This is a friend and parishioner from my church. He's a contractor and has offered to build the stage for our upcoming event. So I figured, why not help a friend and support our work event as well?"

Catherine smiles back at Ms. Christian and gives her a high-five.

"Wow, that's a fantastic idea! It's rare to work for a selfless woman of God in the corporate world. I'm grateful to learn from you."

"Thank you, Catherine. I'm blessed to have you. I prayed for God to send me someone like you. Approval confirmed."

Catherine rises to her feet and hugs Ms. Christian.

Ms. Christian has taught Catherine everything she knows, so she would never doubt or question her instructions. But what Catherine doesn't know is that this will be the approval that seals her fate.

After approving the new vendor, Catherine is consumed with work for the next several days. She and Ms. Christian finalize logistics for an event scheduled for the following weekend. It's always a race to the finish when they are only days away from an event, but their weekly Thursday check-in meetings with the executive landlords keep them focused.

But on this particular Thursday, Catherine asks if she can head home early to rest up for Saturday evening's event, and Ms. Christian obliges. Soon after, Ms. Christian enters the conference room, where she finds five executive landlords—a larger group than usual—sitting facing her as she takes her seat.

"Good afternoon, Ms. Christian. It has come to our attention that we have an open invoice for an unapproved vendor that was signed off on by me. I have never heard of this vendor, and I haven't given you and Catherine a budget for the stage work. Yet somehow we already have a bill for $15K that is past due. Can you explain how this unapproved vendor received my signature and sign-off?"

Ms. Christian is glad Catherine went home early so the executive landlords can only hear her side of the story. Her Christian character and award-winning reputation are on the line.

"Oh my goodness, Jim, I'm so sorry. I'm so embarrassed. This is the vendor and parishioner from my church who put in a bid to work with us, but I told Catherine to hold off on approvals until I spoke with you. She only uses my pre-saved signature on official documents when I don't have time to sign them. I don't know how she obtained yours. This is extremely unprofessional and problematic and not at all something she learned from me."

On the contrary, this is exactly what Catherine learned from Ms. Christian. Forging signatures was part of her training; Ms. Christian had assured her the executive landlords were aware of the process and had approved it for efficiency.

"Forging our signatures on company documents is illegal and could cost us everything. We're going to have to let Catherine go, effective immediately. We will have security gather her things, and she can collect them from the security office tomorrow morning," says Jim.

Ms. Christian drops her head and holds back tears. She's embarrassed and ashamed, but relieved she isn't the one losing her job.

"Understandable. I apologize for my extreme oversight of this matter, everyone."

"Since we are down to the wire with planning, Ms. Christian, we trust you, so let's go with the vendor from your church. He's expensive, but we don't have time to waste. I'll sign off on the invoice and send it through for booking. I will also contact Catherine. Thank you, Ms. Christian. Get some rest."

"I'll try," says Ms. Christian as she wipes the tears away from her cheeks.

Ms. Christian feels dizzy as she rises to her feet. On her walk back to her cubicle, she places a final prayer card on Catherine's desk. "God bless you," she whispers.

Catherine receives an immediate termination notice via email on Thursday evening. Confused and heartbroken, she tries emailing the executive landlords and Ms. Christian for an explanation, but finds that her email address has been blocked. Catherine is later contacted by security to pick up her things at 6:00 a.m. on Friday, before anyone arrives at the office.

Ms. Christian glides into the office on Friday morning as if nothing had happened. Determined to show her parishioner and new vendor her flawless reputation at work, she's excited to do a mock run-of-show and supervise the stage being built before the event the following evening.

As the afternoon approaches, the stage and vendor booths are completed, and Ms. Christian feels accomplished.

On the way to his car, Executive Landlord Jim compliments her on her work and the new stage: "Great work, Ms. Christian! I knew you'd pull it all together flawlessly despite the drama of the last twenty-four hours. This stage looks better than the other stages we've had! It looks sturdy and fresh. Let me get those pieces of plastic for you before I head out."

Jim walks onto the stage toward the pieces of plastic, and suddenly the middle of the stage collapses in front of him, leaving him upright and intact, thank God.

Jim and Ms. Christian freeze in disbelief.

"Um, Ms. Christian, what the FUCK?! I almost died just now! What kind of contractor is this?! Is he even licensed?"

Ms. Christian feels the blood drain from her face.

"I—I—um. No, no. He's not licensed; he told me he was in the process of getting licensed but that he does this work all the time! I see him every Sunday at church with his family! I thought I could trust him!"

Jim cautiously tiptoes down the stairs of the stage like a cat and runs over to her. "That stage almost killed me! Get your vendor back here. He's fired! We are doing this event without a stage, and you will make it work. He's lucky I'm not reporting his business to the Better Business Bureau! No more unapproved vendors moving forward, Ms. Christian."

Ms. Christian's hands begin to shake as the weight of her negligence and dishonesty sets in. She knows this isn't a good time to double down on her mistakes, but she needs to come clean about Catherine. "I understand, Jim. But there's one more thing I need to tell you. Catherine was not to blame for the forging of your signature. That's how I trained her since the first day she was hired. For efficiency purposes, it's just easier to sign your name. I have your signature saved in my files along with the signatures of other executive landlords. She asked me about this vendor because she knew he was unapproved, and I told her to approve him because he was a friend. I'm sorry, Jim."

Jim shakes his head and drops his hands to his sides. "This is incredibly disappointing, Ms. Christian. We trusted you, and you let us down twice this week in costly ways. Please pack up your office and leave the premises. I cannot, in good faith or conscience, have you work another day for this company."

Good faith and good conscience.

These are concepts that don't often exist in the corporate workplace.

Ironically, these were traits everyone thought Ms. Christian had, but in actuality, she didn't. Her lack of sound values and morals ultimately led to her dismissal and a severe hit to her reputation.

But she gained a mindset shift she would not have had if it weren't for the costly mistakes she made.

Catherine received an apology from the executive landlords and was rehired and given a raise. Ms. Christian left the industry entirely, became an entrepreneur, and started a consulting business.

This painful moment served as the breakthrough catalyst for both women to flourish on their own terms.

In the corporate workplace, values and morals are often pushed to the side in the name of success and maintaining a certain level of authority. But if it eats away at your soul and destroys your character, is it success?

No, it's not.

When the opportunity arises to stand up for your colleagues or your team, don't be like Ms. Christian and throw them under the bus to save yourself.

Speak up and tell the truth.

Your humility will speak volumes about your character and integrity, and that is priceless.

Excuse me while I throw this prayer card coaster in the trash, respectfully, and turn the page to Ebony's final story.

• • •

Professional Development
For the Corporate Soul

Shifting from freeze or fawn into flight—a place of thriving—requires redefining success. How do you currently define success in your life and career? Is it aligned with your true values, or are you chasing external recognition?

"I had to realize what I tolerate is optional,
and anything I tell myself is possible."
—GLORILLA, "BETTER THANGS" REMIX

____

____

____

____

____

____

Conclusion

I know you've got your hot tea ready to sip for the next story, but I hate to break it to you. We're at the end.

Thank you for keeping up with me, staying hydrated, and following my lead as we moved through my *Corporate Mute* journey.

You trusted me through the sunny days and quiet storms as we put on our not-so-rose-colored glasses. We laughed, cried, sweated (a lot), danced, side-eyed executive landlords and workplace hype machines, ate bland and upscale lunches, took deep breaths, journaled, and unclenched our jaws after the turbulence, easing into a soft landing and the final shift of this journey.

I wasn't lying when I said these corporate workplace streets were rugged and thugged out, right? *Pewn pewn!*

As we close, I've taken the time to reflect on all the personalities I've encountered—and even sometimes embodied—to survive the corporate healthcare world: Ms. Brain Fog, Ms. Lowball, Ms. Searching, Ms. Secretary, Ms. Compliment, Ms. No-Degree, Ms. People-Pleaser, Ms. Event Planner, and Ms. Christian.

And what did I find in these experiences? My role.

For over twenty years, I've had to shapeshift, transition, and adapt through countless personas to remain resilient in the face of adversity—ultimately emerging as a stronger, more compassionate leader who has both mentored others and been mentored along the way.

That role continues to take shape with every lesson learned. These lessons have been instrumental in both Ebony's journey and mine, grounded in leading by example, standing up to injustice, and treating colleagues as partners to learn and grow with rather than subordinates to manage.

Every workplace benefits from leadership rooted in integrity, growth, and accountability, and I'm grateful to have learned from— and grown alongside—the best and worst examples of it.

It's only right that I conclude *The Corporate Mute* with a jammin' song, and it's a song that has divinely resurfaced in my mind and heart as I close.

In 1978, Chaka Khan released her debut solo single, "I'm Every Woman," from her first album, *Chaka*.

The song gained further popularity in 1993 with Whitney Houston's remixed version, released as the second single from *The Bodyguard* soundtrack album (1992).

"I'm Every Woman" is an iconic and timeless song that celebrates the individual and collective strength, diversity, and resilience of women.

But it's more than a song.

It's an anthem.

I want *The Corporate Mute* to be a living, breathing anthem for women in the corporate workplace, because my stories are our stories.

I can't sing—or "sang"—like Whitney or Chaka, but I hope that after reading my stories, you feel seen, understood, and reminded of our shared experiences and joy as women.

And whenever you begin to doubt yourself or feel overwhelmed by the corporate workplace, know that you can "press play" on *The Corporate Mute* and remind yourself that you are not alone.

My journey through Freeze, Fawn, and Flight was tough, and it almost broke me.

Almost.

But I'm tougher, and so are you.

When I look at myself in the mirror now, I'm no longer asking myself, *Who am I? How do people perceive me? Am I being fake?* I see a beautiful woman who is confident in who she is and whose she is, taking every step unapologetically and unashamedly with authenticity, love, acceptance, peace, and joy.

But I wouldn't be that woman today without every persona I embodied to survive and eventually thrive, and I hope each one taught you a rich lesson.

As we close this final chapter of *The Corporate Mute*, this isn't a goodbye but a see you very soon!

I don't want our conversations or stories to end here—Ebony's journey is far from over.

Her saga continues on *The Corporate Mute* blog page, where she shares more stories and invites you to share yours too! Who knows? Your story may be featured on her blog!

Oh, and one more thing.

There's more to Ebony's life than just the corporate workplace.

Think Ebony's stories can't get any more wildly hilarious or complicated? The plot thickens and expands as we explore other facets of her world, like the church, her sorority, and more.

If you enjoyed *The Corporate Mute*, you don't want to miss this!

Connect soon!

References

National September 11 Memorial & Museum. Module 1: Events of
the Day. Accessed March 24, 2025, https://www.911memorial.
org/learn/resources/911-primer/module-1-events-day

Hartig, Hannah, and Carroll Doherty. "Two Decades Later, the
Enduring Legacy of 9/11." Pew Research Center. September
2, 2021, https://www.pewresearch.org/politics/2021/09/02/
two-decades-later-the-enduring-legacy-of-9-11/

About the Author

Tiffany Gray Jackson, a proud native of Memphis, Tennessee, holds a Master of Public Administration from Strayer University and is deeply rooted in purpose. Inspired by her grandmother's decades-long dedication to the nursing profession and patient care, Tiffany has dedicated her career to improving people's lives and creating meaningful impact in professional environments. 

After only a short time into her career, Tiffany realized that the corporate space was not always built for people who looked like her: an unashamed, unapologetic, highly educated, talented, driven, and ridiculously fly African American woman.

Tiffany's debut title, *The Corporate Mute*, is her comedic and insightful take on workplace dynamics and experiences, highlighting common themes and colorful personas encountered in professional environments through a fictional narrative inspired by real-world experiences.

Tiffany's life mission is to spark change in others, fueled by the strength and resilience cultivated through every rise, fall, and shift she has encountered along the way. Her story is far from over, and her journey continues.

In her spare time, Tiffany enjoys streaming classic movies with her husband (alongside a big bowl of popcorn with hot sauce and an ice-cold Coke), weekly Mexican food and mango margarita nights with family and friends, and attending leadership conferences.

Learn more about Tiffany by scanning here.